ENCYCLOPEDIA FOR KIDS
GREAT INVENTORS AND INVENTIONS IN HISTORY

Children's Ecology Books

All Rights reserved. No part of this book may be reproduced or used in any way or form or by any means whether electronic or mechanical, this means that you cannot record or photocopy any material ideas or tips that are provided in this book.

Copyright 2016

GENIUS ACTS!

LET'S TAKE ADVANTAGE OF THE FINEST MINDS IN HISTORY!

In this book, you will be introduced to great inventors and inventions in history.

These brilliant minds made our lives easier today!

ARCHIMEDES OF SYRACUSE

Meet the greatest mathematician of all time!

He calculated the value of pi and figured out how to determine the area under the arc of a parabola.

He invented cool machines, including siege weapons for armies. He invented the water screw and the lever. Our basic tools like scissors, pliers, hammer claws, nutcrackers and tongs use levers he invented.

NIKOLA TESLA

Meet one of the most innovative minds in history!

He was responsible for the birth of commercial electricity.

He laid the foundation for the development of the remote control, the use of radar and the field of computer science. He contributed much to the science of robotics.

THOMAS EDISON

Meet the most prolific inventor in modern history!

He invented the light bulb, the phonograph, the motion picture camera, and many other useful and obscure gadgets.

This gifted man literally electrified New York City. He is one of the great inventors of the nineteenth century.

ALEXANDER GRAHAM BELL

Meet another genius in history!

He was most famous for the invention of the telephone. He also invented the modern metal detector.

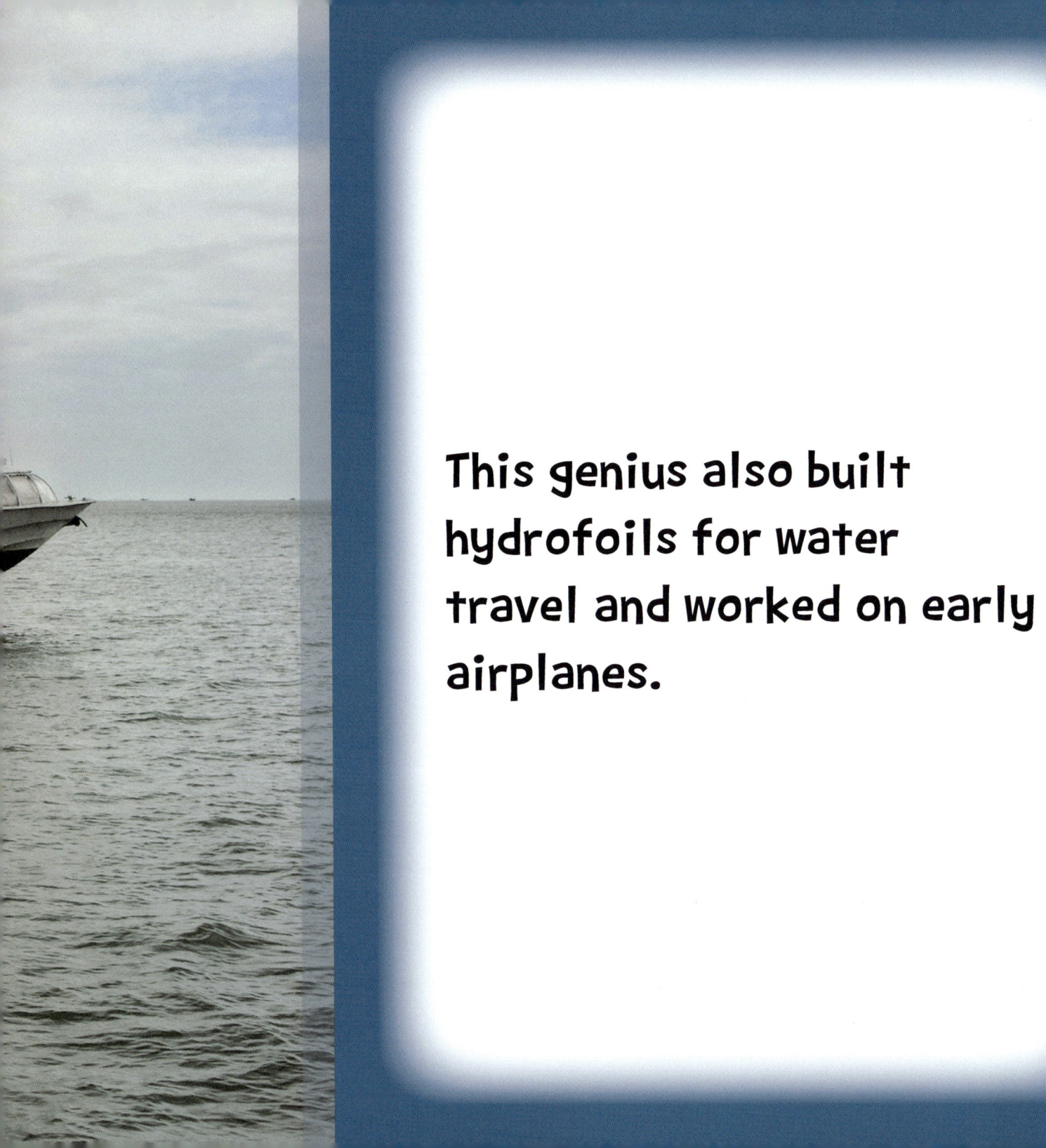

This genius also built hydrofoils for water travel and worked on early airplanes.

GEORGE WESTINGHOUSE

Meet the prolific inventor and engineer!

Westinghouse's contributions paralleled Edison's inventions. His electrical system, which used alternating current instead of direct current made him famous.

His AC power system is one of his great inventions. He also invented the railway air brake.

JEROME "JERRY" HAL LEMELSON

Meet one of the most prolific inventors in history!

Among his great inventions were automated warehouses, cordless telephones, industrial robots,

videocassette recorders, fax machines, camcorders and the magnetic tape drive used in Sony's Walkman tape players. He is the champion of the independent inventor's community.

He filed patents for cancer detection and treatment, consumer electronics, television, and diamond coating technologies.

HERO OF ALEXANDRIA

Meet one of the finest minds in the Roman Empire!

His most famous invention is the Aeolipile, which is a primordial steam engine.

It can spin a metal ball. His other inventions include force pumps, the first syringe, a fountain to create hydrostatic electricity, a windmill operated organ, and the first coin operated machine. All these happened during the pre-industrial age.

BENJAMIN FRANKLIN

Meet the prodigious inventor!

He created the lightning rod, the glass armonica, the Franklin stove, bifocal glasses, the carriage odometer and the urinary catheter.

CAI LUN

Meet the great Chinese inventor!

He is an inventor of modern paper and the paper-making process. He used raw materials in his inventions. These materials include bark, hemp, silk, and fishing net.

THE WRIGHT BROTHERS

Meet the great American inventors!

In 1903, they successfully designed, built and flew the first powered aircraft.

CHARLES BABBAGE

Meet the English mathematician and inventor!

He invented the first mechanical computer. He is considered as the Father of Computers.

These famous inventions have made our lives easier!

In other words, today's conveniences are the results of the great inventions of the past.

We thank the great inventors who have shared and contributed their brilliance to humankind.

Printed in Great Britain
by Amazon